D0942249

The Guide to
Plants for the Reptile Terrarium

Jerry G. Walls
Photos by Maleta M. Walls

HOUSTON PUBLIC LIBRARY

R01149 69910

CONTENTS

TILLANDSIA IONANTHA ON DECORATIVE BASE

RE 157

Our thanks to Hagerty the Florist, Cranbury, NJ, for the run of their greenhouses

To the memory of Alvin, who liked plants in his own simple way

© T.F.H. Publications, Inc.

Distributed in the UNITED STATES to the Pet Trade by T.F.H. Publications, Inc., 1 TFH Plaza, Neptune City, NJ 07753; on the Internet at www.tfh.com; in CANADA by Rolf C. Hagen Inc., 3225 Sartelon St., Montreal, Quebec H4R 1E8; Pet Trade by H & L Pet Supplies Inc., 27 Kingston Crescent, Kitchener, Ontario N2B 2T6; in ENGLAND by T.F.H. Publications, PO Box 74, Havant PO9 5TT; in AUSTRALIA AND THE SOUTH PACIFIC by T.F.H. (Australia), Pty. Ltd., Box 149, Brookvale 2100 N.S.W., Australia; in NEW ZEALAND by Brooklands Aquarium Ltd., 5 McGiven Drive, New Plymouth, RD1 New Zealand; in SOUTH AFRICA by Rolf C. Hagen S.A. (PTY.) LTD., P.O. Box 201199, Durban North 4016, South Africa; in JAPAN by T.F.H. Publications, Japan—Jiro Tsuda, 10-12-3 Ohjidai, Sakura, Chiba 285, Japan. Published by T.F.H. Publications, Inc.
MANUFACTURED IN THE
UNITED STATES OF AMERICA
BY T.F.H. PUBLICATIONS, INC.

INTRODUCTION

I must admit that I approached writing this book with some apprehension. The topic of terrarium plants is a broad one, yet it seldom has been treated in the American hobby literature. In Germany and the other European countries there is a well-developed segment of terrarium care dealing with not only the plants for the terrarium but the ways to design a terrarium to suit a particular point of view. Entire books have been written on the subject of specialized terraria, terrarium construction and design, and "super terraria" with all the latest technological advances in light, heat, and humidity control.

Perhaps fortunately, this book is designed to just give the average hobbyist an introduction to the many plants that are suitable for use in the terrarium. I will not concern myself here with terrarium design or the controversy of whether plants and animals must always agree as to the areas from which they originated. (Many European hobbyists would laugh out loud if they saw a group of Chinese evergreens, *Aglaonema*, decorating a terrarium with South American poison frogs, dendrobatids. They feel that to mix plants and animals from different continents, or even different ecological regions within a continent, is a major faux pas that would never be committed by a serious hobbyist. So far American terrarium hobbyists have not adopted this view, though it recently has become more common in the aquarium hobby.) What I will try to do is put you on speaking terms with about four or five dozen readily available plants that are suitable for decorating various types of terraria. Many people, including

If you really want to use living plants in your terrarium, you have an almost limitless choice. *Acalypha* sp., a chenille plant, is just one of many species suitable for a humid but bright terrarium.

me, find care of living plants difficult even on the kitchen or living room windowsill, and the thought of trying to maintain five or six different plants in a small container strikes fear in their heart. If you have a real "black thumb," you might want to read the section on artificial plants. I hope, however, that the next chapter will give you enough information on basic plant care to get you started on at least a simply planted terrarium.

WHY PLANTS?

Are there any real reasons why you should strive for a planted terrarium? Certainly the animals themselves don't seem to know or care what surrounds them in the cage. A treefrog seems just as contented sitting on a plastic plant as on a living one. Living plants have many problems when you try to put them into a small glass box, and it is difficult to match the various degrees of light, heat, and humidity, as well as substrate types, that keep a plant healthy with similar factors that make an animal happy.

There is no doubt that the human eye enjoys a well-planted terrarium. It seems more natural and appropriate for a herp to be in a green background than one of paper towels and plain rocks. However, terrarium plants do nothing to promote the long-term health of the pet herp. Unlike their role in aquaria, they do not provide oxygen, hopefully will not be eaten by the herps, and do little to change the physical parameters in the terrarium (except perhaps stabilizing humidity).

Planted terraria seem to me to exist for two simple reasons, both dealing with the psychology of the keeper rather than of the kept. First, keepers just enjoy the appearance of a planted terrarium, feeling it makes their animals more beautiful in natural-like surroundings. Second, many hobbyists just enjoy the challenge of keeping plants alive under what must be called extremely difficult circumstances. They enjoy the thrill of designing a lighting system that will keep both a low-light and a bright-light plant healthy in the same terrarium. For these hobbyists a planted terrarium is just one more step up the ladder to becoming a "serious

Chinese evergreens, *Aglaonema*, originated in tropical Asia. Would they be out of place in a terrarium with South American herps?

hobbyist" rather than an "amateur."

Should you bother to plant your terrarium? I believe the answer is yes, at least in moderation. Personally, I think the herp hobby is about keeping and perhaps breeding reptiles and amphibians. It is not about keeping plants in enclosed containers, which is a segment of horticulture, not herpetoculture. Using plants as decorative elements to improve the appearance of the terrarium is fine, and there certainly is no harm is trying your hand at both some simple green terrarium inhabitants and a few more difficult charges such as cacti and perhaps an orchid or two. When you begin to spend more time keeping the plants than the animals and design the terrarium so the light and humidity are more suitable for orchids than for treefrogs, you have moved into another hobby. There is nothing wrong with this, but it certainly is beyond the realm of what I hope to cover in this book.

A WORD ON NAMES

A word of explanation about the names used for the plants in this book is in order. As in the animal kingdom, the scientific names of plants are controlled by a set of quite strict rules that must be followed by scientists working in botany. However, horticulturists, who might be considered practical botanists, have never felt constrained to follow the technical rules in all their details. For one thing, many of the plants sold in nurseries are not species, but instead are hybrids of various types, sometimes between genera (especially in orchids and cacti), or selectively bred color or leaf-form varieties (cultivars) that are reproduced by cuttings and not sexually through seeds. Such horticultural varieties often bear horticultural names, which is only appropriate, and these fall outside the codes used for scientific names. In this book I will be emphasizing only the genera of selected plants, with a few casual mentions of species and cultivar names. It must be understood that the scientific names used here are those of convenience and the ones most often used in the horticultural literature available to me. In many cases scientific reviews of the genera and species in question would determine that different names should be used, because botanical nomenclature is no more stable than is zoological nomenclature. Common names for plants also vary

Names are subject to change in plants as they are in animals. Identifications often also are a problem, as many terrarium plants rarely flower. Finding differences between plants of *Scindapsus aureus* (also known as *Eupremnum aureum*) and *Philodendron scandens* (right) is difficult.

The quality of artificial plants has improved, and some, such as these false *Philodendron scandens*, are extremely life-like. Good artificial plants may cost more than living plants but often last longer. Herps seldom can tell the difference between live and fake.

tremendously, and in the case of horticultural plants a group of nurseries may use different names from year to year—customers buy new names faster than old names. I've tried to give multiple common names whenever possible.

ARTIFICIAL PLANTS

If you have a "black thumb," then perhaps you should stick with artificial plants rather than kill living things. Remember, your pets will not care whether a plant is living or plastic and fabric, and they won't notice the difference unless they try to eat it. There are some truly nice artificial plants available today that look almost as real as living greenery and don't require balancing acts of light, heat, and humidity.

Try your pet shop first when looking for artificials. More and more shops today are carrying

some good plastics at reasonable prices. Artificials can be found in many other types of stores, from large department stores to craft

Don't get carried away with bright colors in artificial plants—keep with the life-like types. This false coleus (the real plant demands too much light for the terrarium) looks nice in a terrarium.

stores. The only restrictions are that to be usable an artificial plant must be color-fast and sturdy. An artificial does not have to be pre-mounted on a base, as a bit of wire or cloth tape will allow you to attach leaves and segments of stems to basking branches, the edges of water dishes, artificial cliff faces, etc.

Try to get a good variety of plastic foliage types when you buy your plants. Provide a few large, stiff leaves as resting perches and possible egg-laying sites for frogs, some sprays of greenery with a few more colorful leaves as cover in the corners of the terrarium, and perhaps a few loose viney types for hanging from the back of the terrarium. Large centerpieces should be subdued. Stay away from artificial flowers, as they always look fake if they are placed in good light near the front of the terrarium.

Don't be afraid to cut artificials into the lengths you need and regroup them into the types of pieces you need. A few large green leaves look nice, for instance, hanging over the edge of a water bowl and also give stupid crickets a ramp to try to leave the water after their daily swim. Eggs laid on artificial leaves can easily be removed to a brooder jar for safe incubation. A small wirecutter, florist tape, and wires of various types and sizes should be kept on hand.

Before you put the artificials in the terrarium, test them for color-fastness by running hot water over them for a few minutes. If the water turns green, of course the piece should be used only with caution, and preferably in a terrarium with limited humidity. All plastic plants should be taken out of the terrarium regularly and washed thoroughly under hot water to remove dust and feces, then dipped in bleach and carefully rinsed and dried. Even strong bleach solutions have little effect on most artificials.

You will find that good artificial plants cost about the same as small living plants, though of course they last a lot longer and are more versatile. In some types of terraria, such as very dry setups with herbivorous lizards, you may be able to support only artificial plants.

CORK AND CHOLLA

Two common decorative items in many terraria are plant

Cacti are woody plants, and they have skeletons under their outer tissue and spines. Cholla (pronounced choy-a) wood is produced from dead, cleaned *Opuntia* segments.

Cork bark is produced by systematic stripping of orchards of a special European oak tree. The product is one of the most useful in decorating the terrarium.

products that should be of interest to hobbyists. The elaborate networks of wooden fibers that often are used in desert terraria are the woody skeletons of various types of cacti usually called cholla (pronounced choy–a). These usually are cylindrical species of *Opuntia*, the gigantic genus of cacti so familiar in the American Southwest. Though most *Opuntia* have flattened, rounded segments (bunny-ears), in the cholla group the segments are close to cylindrical and often are weakly attached to each other. When you pass near a living cholla (and even a dead one for that matter), the slightest brush against it causes a segment to break loose and literally attack you with its hundreds of spines.

Prepared cholla as seen in the pet shop is either collected dead or is harvested and then treated to remove the living tissue and leave only the woody fibers that supported the cactus in life. The skeleton has been carefully cleaned and often bleached to present an attractive appearance. For some reason cholla most often is used in terraria for tarantulas and lizards, but it also is a nice decoration for any dry terrarium. A major problem with cholla is that many animals like to crawl into the hollow center and wedge themselves, becoming impossible to remove when you want them out.

Cork is the product of a Mediterranean oak tree, *Quercus suber*. This evergreen oak has been utilized since prehistoric times for its renewable bark that contains numerous tiny air-filled cells that allow it to float. A cubic inch of natural cork bark contains over 20 million cells, resulting in the bark having a specific gravity only one-quarter that of water; i.e., it floats and floats high in the water. The air-filled cells also serve as excellent insulation from heat.

The cork oak primarily is harvested in Spain and Portugal and to a lesser extent in northern Africa. Portugal provides about 50% of the cork harvested, while Spain provides another 28%. Each cork oak, which may live to over 150 years if everything goes right, can be stripped of its bark in carefully planned sequences about a dozen times during its life, producing a truly renewable agricultural crop. Much of the stripping of the bark is still done manually using hand tools, but the industry (including all the processed cork products used in manufacturing) is reported to be worth over 300 million dollars.

Cork used in the terrarium generally is in the form of natural cork bark. This represents pieces of oak bark that simply have been removed from a tree, washed, and dried. Often cork bark still has lichens and other small plants attached to it, increasing its interest and individuality in the terrarium. It is easily cut with a small jigsaw or handsaw and even can be broken apart by hand. Commonly the pieces available are anywhere from 2 or 3 inches in diameter to well over a foot and from 1 to 4 feet in length. Cork bark usually is sold by the pound and is a very cheap, attractive, and useful plant to always have on hand in the reptile room. It can be used for hideboxes, as background logs, and even cut and overlapped to cover an otherwise uninteresting wall in the terrarium. It also provides a very attractive part of many photographic backgrounds. Few plant products are more versatile

Sand-blasted grape roots (*Vitis* sp.) come in bizarre shapes and, though expensive, make excellent additions to the terrarium.

and useful in the terrarium.

Finally, a brief mention of two plant products that recently have become widely available to the terrarium market. One is sand-blasted grapevine, assumedly *Vitis*. These gnarled, tangled woody stems and roots are each completely individual and lend a distinctive touch to any terrarium. Manzanita, the blackish red wood from a small southwestern tree or shrub, sometimes appears on the market and makes an excellent perch or just decorative background. The varied diameters of a typical piece work well for chameleons and tree boas.

SPHAGNUM AND PEAT

Sphagnum moss is a true moss, any of the many species of the genus *Sphagnum*, family Sphagnaceae. There are well over 50 species in North America, and the genus occurs over much of the Earth. It tends to grow in dense mats along moist stream edges, near ponds, and especially in acid bogs. The leaves and stems have many gigantically enlarged hollow cells that have the ability to absorb a tremendous amount of water. Sphagnum moss is the term usually applied to the living moss and the long-fiber cleaned product that represents the moss in its nearly natural state. Where sphagnum occurs in bogs, it often has been there in large populations for thousands of years, each generation dying and being buried by the next generation. Because the acid water in the bog prevents decomposition of the moss, and because the moss itself seems to have various chemicals that keep it together, over the years it builds up yard after yard of compressed dead moss. This material still looks something like the original moss but generally is a dark brown to nearly black color. This is peat moss, and it is produced by mining a peat bog. Often the peat is dug out by manual labor and produced in the form of peat bricks, but today it tends to be dug out with backhoes and processed into bales in peat mines. Once dried, peat moss becomes crumbly and is easily pounded into a fine powder that serves as an excellent addition to potting media because it is a rich organic material.

Sphagnum moss is available as loose long strands of green moss in dried form and also as sheets that tend to hold their form. Sphagnum often is placed over gravel at the base of a terrarium before the soil or sand is added. It has a reputation as a great waste cleaner and disinfectant (it has been used for bandages and compresses and seems to reduce risk of infections). Sheets of sphagnum absorb a large amount of water and serve as a fine base for small amphibians in addition to having a very natural appearance in the terrarium and reviving well under low light. The living moss can be collected locally in many areas (though large-scale collecting may be controlled).

Peat moss is available as long cleaned brown strands, as small rounded pearls, as a dry dust-like powder, and probably in many other forms. It even is molded into planting pots and small compressed plates that blossom into small pots when soaked. It absorbs a great amount of water much like the living or freshly dead moss and takes a long time to decompose. There are few potting mixes for non-desert plants that do not use peat moss in one form or another.

That dry brown powder you purchase as peat for potting your plants once was a living green moss, *Sphagnum* sp., whose cell structure allows it to hold tremendous amounts of water.

BASIC PLANT CARE

The care of plants is if anything more complex than the care of animals. Animals usually can move themselves out of an unsuitable environment into conditions that are more bearable, while plants are anchored to one spot. A plant is dependent on the details of its environment to survive, the microhabitat. It reacts to how and when the light hits it and in what quantities as well as the nature of the soil and the air that surround it. Plants can move their leaves a bit and change the way in which they interact with the light, much like reptiles align their bodies to make best use of sunlight for basking.

Because a plant is anchored in position, it is dependent on your knowledge in placing it in the terrarium and then maintaining conditions that allow it to survive. There is a whole library of plant care books that can provide you with details of how to take care of almost any plant, and the entire science of horticulture exists to study the relationships between plants and their captive conditions. Space limitations allow me to mention only a few of the more important aspects of care that apply to terrarium plants. These aspects include lighting, watering and atmospheric humidity, and general physical care such as potting and repotting. For more

Knowing how a plant reacts to water is important in keeping it alive in the terrarium. The broad green leaves of *Saintpaulia ionantha*, the African Violet, look good in a terrarium, but they die or at least turn brown if water drops onto them. Some plants need water only from the roots, but others require heavy misting.

detailed information, check your local library for appropriate gardening books.

LIGHTING

When you think of plants, you think of light. Lighting is very important in the care of terrarium reptiles and amphibians, and it therefore serves as a great restriction on the keeping of plants as secondary living things in a terrarium. You will not be willing to change the lights to support a certain plant if it means that the herps cannot thrive.

Lighting generally is of three types: sunlight, incandescent, and fluorescent. (We'll ignore the high-tech mercury vapor and other high-intensity lighting systems now used by some terrarium hobbyists; they require expensive power supplies and usually run too hot for most plants.) Sunlight is of course natural light and it is immensely powerful. During the summer, bright sunlight at midday in the Northern Hemisphere may register at 10,000 or more foot-candles of light. (A foot-candle is the uniform light cast by a standard candle at a distance of one foot. Stated a different way, 1 foot-candle is 1 lumen per square foot; one lux, a still different measurement of light, is equal to 1 lumen per square yard.) That same sunlight at a bright window is reduced to only 4,000 or 5,000 foot-candles, while just a few feet further into the house it drops sharply to only 400 or fewer foot-candles. You can read a printed page without eyestrain in just 50 foot-candles

The standard lighting for terrarium plants is a bank of two 4-foot fluorescent bulbs. Ordinary shop lights work well and are inexpensive, but many complicated and highly efficient lighting systems also are available.

of light.

Plants are not too choosy about the quality of the light they receive unless they are preparing to flower. We are concerned in this book mostly with foliage plants, those grown for their leaves or overall form, flowers being a secondary consideration, so for terrarium purposes a plant doesn't care too much whether we are using incandescent (tungsten filament) or fluorescent lighting. I'll make the assumption that your basic lighting in a planted terrarium will be fluorescent, perhaps with spotlights available to emphasize interesting plants and to serve as basking lights for the herps.

Light tolerance is important in positioning plants in the habitat. Most ferns, such as this Christmas Fern, *Polystichum acrostichoides*, a common native, require shade and die when exposed to intense light.

Fluorescent lights generally are used in pairs, a bank, placed in a shallow reflector. If you are planning on growing plants in the terrarium, you are well-advised to start with one bank of lights extending from end to end of the terrarium. Wattage of fluorescents is a factor of length, with tubes 4 feet long being rated at 40 watts. In most of the light gardening and horticultural literature a standard bank of lights is a fixture 4 feet long with two tubes. These can be either warm white, cool white, one of each (for the best appearance of the plants to the eye), or plant growing lights; full-spectrum reptile fluorescents also are fine for plants, and since they are the type usually used in herp terraria they will have to do for the plants as well. Remember, herps come first.

The intensity of the light (in foot-candles or lux) diminishes rapidly with distance from the light. Fluorescents provide a very diffuse light that weakens not only in vertical distance from the light but also in lateral distance from the center of the tubes. For example, a bank of 40-watt lights will produce about 850 foot-candles of light directly under the center of the lights at 6 inches, 500 at 1 foot below, 250 at 2 feet, and only 100 at 3 feet. The same bank will produce about 60% as many foot-candles at 6 inches below the tubes but only 6 inches to either side of center.

What this means in practical terrarium terms is that a plant placed directly under a bank of lamps, with its base about 2 feet

A plant stand with adjustable lighting and trays is an excellent way of giving your plants a "vacation" from the turmoil and marginal conditions in the terrarium. Virtually all plants need several weeks of relaxation for every few months in the terrarium.

below the tubes (not unreasonable) and growing upward will have available to it only some 250 to 800 foot-candles of light. Compared to the 10,000 foot-candles in a summer garden at mid-day, this is trivial, but it is enough for many plants to thrive in the terrarium. These low-light plants often come from tropical rain forests where they grow in heavily shaded sites below large trees or as vines and epiphytes (plants whose roots do not grow into the soil for nutriment) in dense forests.

Low-light plants will form the majority of plants that can be kept in the terrarium, but some plants that like brighter light can be kept if a spotlight is focused on them. A 150-watt spotlight with a built-in reflector can provide over 1,000 foot-candles of light at 2 feet in the terrarium. Their intensity drops off to the sides even faster than in fluorescent tubes, however, and just 1 foot to either side of center a spotlight will provide less than 100 foot-candles of light.

Both fluorescent and incandescent lamps produce heat, but fluorescents are relatively cool. A spotlight focused on a plant at just 2 or 3 feet could easily burn the plant and cause its quick death, while a bank of fluorescents will provide only moderate heating of the air and the plant. Fluorescents should always be your first choice for lighting a planted terrarium, with spotlights being used judiciously to accent plants. Remember that you will have reptiles or amphibians in the terrarium and they may be even more sensitive to air temperatures than the plants. At least a pair of thermometers, one at substrate level and one near the top of the terrarium, is a must in a large planted terrarium.

Virtually all plants require about 12 to 14 hours of light per day during their growing season, reduced considerably during the several months when they would either be subjected to low winter temperatures (in the temperate zone) or a dry season (in the tropics). In most cases you will be able to time a plant's resting period to match that of the reptiles kept in the same terrarium, but in other instances you will have to remove the plant from the terrarium to a relatively cool or dry area for a few months. I'll try to mention such details in the plant accounts, but it might be safest to always plan on not letting a single plant remain in the terrarium for more than six months before removing it for rest and relaxation.

WATER IN POTS AND THE AIR

The confined habitat of the terrarium is very hard on a plant because it is difficult to provide a good balance of water coming in through the roots and water in the air. Often the soil around the roots becomes very dry, while the air is constantly saturated. During the winter in the Northern Hemisphere most houses have very low atmospheric humidity (often only 10 to 20% saturation, and certainly less than 50%).

Successful terrarium plants are those that can adapt to great variations in water levels above and below. The terrarium keeper can control these conditions somewhat by careful watering and potting protocols.

First, pots. Because individual plants seldom do well in the terrarium for long periods, it is best to place each plant (except for some of the low-growing ground cover types) in a separate pot of more or less standard size and just bury the pot in the substrate. This allows you to arrange for proper drainage by placing pebbles and shards at the bottom of the pot. Otherwise you will have to put a layer of gravel over the bottom of the terrarium first before adding the substrate. Two basic types of pots are available, plastic and clay. Clay pots are porous and allow water to enter from outside while excess water escapes not only through the drainage hole at the bottom but also slowly diffuses through the sides if the soil becomes too wet. Plastic pots do not allow water to move through them, which can be either an advantage or a disadvantage. Plants in plastic have to be watered less often, but it also is easier to drown a plant with just a bit of extra water.

In the terrarium the best potting method might be the traditional double-pot technique. In this method a clay pot containing the plant is placed within a slightly larger plastic pot that is the one buried in the terrarium substrate. The plant is put in a normal clay pot with a layer of pebbles or broken clay pot shards at the bottom and an appropriate potting mix is added. Be sure to use a clay pot with a drainage hole at the bottom. The larger plastic outer pot should lack a hole, but it should have the usual inch or so of loose pebbles and shards at the bottom. The clay pot is placed within the plastic pot and the space between the two is filled with peat moss. The plant is watered by adding water to the peat moss and letting it diffuse as required into the clay pot.

Plants that have been over-watered tend to lose their leaves from the base. Usually they turn yellow and drop off, but sometimes they just suddenly die. You've drowned the roots and the plant is suffocating. If you under-water a plant, the leaves tend to shrivel first before dropping off. Younger, smaller leaves with thinner surface waxy coats will die first. If you over-water, you may be able to salvage the plant by removing it to a new pot with fresh soil after first carefully knocking off all the old, water-logged soil. The plant probably will die anyway, but at least you tried. Dry plants may be salvaged by removing their pot to the sink or a bowl of water and submersing them to the pot rim for a few minutes. After that let them sit for a few hours before returning to the terrarium. It might be simpler to have correctly potted plants always ready to replace accident victims while they are being given first aid.

Over-watering is more dangerous than under-watering, and it is best to always err on the dry side. The amount of water of course depends on the type of plant being kept. Those in a moist terrarium may require weekly watering, while those of a dry desert terrarium may not require watering for several months at a time.

Atmospheric water (humidity) is more difficult to regulate. Most plants kept in rainforest or meadow terraria need 50% or higher humidity most of the year. During a typical day the temperature in the terrarium will vary quite a bit, dropping at night. The nighttime drop increases the humidity in the terrarium (dew) and helps duplicate natural cycles. Moisture in the soil will be moved to the air by evaporation from leaves, increasing air moisture. Additionally, daily or twice-daily misting of a terrarium will provide sufficient humidity to make the plants comfortable. Be sure that you *mist*, not spray with large droplets. Few plants do well if there is water sitting on their leaves for hours at a time, and they will develop black or brown spots and lose their leaves. A very fine mist is necessary.

In a terrarium that must remain moist, you will lose a lot of humidity through a mesh tank lid. In such cases a sheet of glass or plastic over the terrarium will help control the humidity. If the moisture level rises so much that condensation from the top causes problems (remember that plants dislike water droplets on their leaves), pull the glass back a few inches to allow evaporation and a drop in humidity.

TEMPERATURES

Disregarding cacti and certain other succulents, most plants are comfortable at about 60 to 75°F (16 to 24°C), with a ten-degree drop at night. This range can be pushed a bit to about 85°F with little stress on the plant. Thus, most plants can adapt to the temperature range in most terraria (except near the basking light if one is used). With adult plants there is little truth to the business about warm roots promoting growth, and in the terrarium there should be relatively little difference between substrate temperatures and those of the air. The lights will produce a lot of heat, and you probably will be using heat tapes or something similar to heat the bottom of the terrarium as well. Long periods of sustained moist heat are not good for most plants, another reason to give specimens a relaxation period every few months.

FEEDING

In the garden or the kitchen windowsill, plants should be fertilized at regular intervals. This may not be the best course of action in the terrarium, however. Fertilizers are rated by their amount of nitrogen, phosphorus, and potassium, and plant fertilizers state the relative parts of each of these basic nutrients by a standard formula following the same sequence of elements. Nitrogen promotes rapid leaf growth (soft tissue growth), while

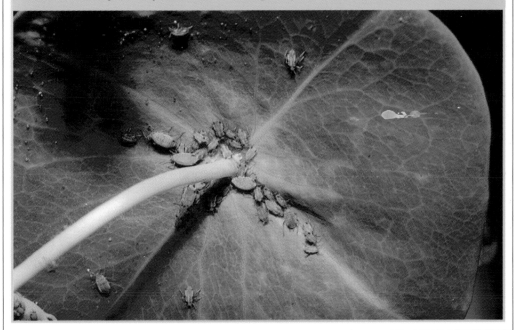

Though there was not room to mention them in the text, be aware that the same pests that attack your house plants, such as aphids, may thrive in the confines of the terrarium. Always treat pests *after* removing the plant from the terrarium.

phosphorus is essential for cellular growth and potassium helps control development. For general purposes, nitrogen and potassium should be present at the same levels, with twice as much phosphorus. A good basic plant fertilizer would be some multiple of the ratio 1 part nitrogen, 2 parts phosphorus, and 1 part potassium (1:2:1).

Unfortunately, compounds with high levels of nitrogen often are poisonous to reptiles and amphibians. Even if fertilizer is added to a terrarium plant at a very low level (half or a quarter of the concentration recommended on the fertilizer label), it could cause poisoning and death of a curious herp that licked the chemical off leaves or even dug into the moistened substrate. If you use a good potting soil mix with a bit of bone meal added and perhaps some additional peat moss, your plants should survive for several months without fertilization, using the nutrients in the soil. Keep a record of when a plant is potted in fresh soil and remove it from the terrarium at least every six months for repotting in fresh mix and fertilization. Plant fertilizers also may be toxic to humans, especially children, and should be kept away from casual handling.

SELECTION

The types of plants you use in your terrarium will of course have to be determined by the terrarium itself (rain forest, woodland, desert, etc.) as well as by the availability of specific plants. Two types of plants, cacti and orchids, require very specialized care if they are to survive, while the bromeliads or air plants also are different enough from regular plants to be treated separately. Most of what you will be adding to the typical terrarium will be foliage plants, those grown for their attractive leaves rather than flowers. Almost any nursery (and recently some pet shops) will stock literally dozens, perhaps over a hundred, different foliage plants in a variety of sizes and suitable for different growing conditions. Most plants are relatively cheap to purchase when small, and they grow rapidly. Furnishing your terrarium with the right plants should not be too expensive, but it can be a lot of fun.

The following chapters consider several dozen plants of varied types that are suitable for terraria, but not all may be available locally; many also are seasonally available. If a plant is cheap enough, the right size for your needs, and doesn't seem to be too different in requirements from the conditions in your terrarium, don't be afraid to experiment. Remember that most plants in a nursery are adapted to rather high light requirements and will grow best if exposed to several hours of direct sunlight each day—this is of course almost impossible in the terrarium, though a spotlight may help, but you usually can gradually wean a plant from bright light conditions to more subdued lighting over a few days or weeks.

BROMELIADS, THE AIR PLANTS

When we speak of air plants, we are talking about epiphytes, plants that are able to sustain themselves without a root system and often attach to other living plants for support. Though epiphytes occur in many plant families (the familiar mistletoes of Christmas fame are broad-leaved epiphtyes that also parasitize their host trees), the dominant group of epiphytes is the bromeliads, family Bromeliaceae. This large (2,000 and more species, with many described as new each year) family is strictly American (except for one isolated species in Africa), being abundantly represented in the floras from Mexico to central South America. In cool, humid cloud forests of the various mountain ranges they may be the dominant plants, but they also occur along the seacoast of Brazil and on the arid, rocky mountains of Chile.

Though some of the species have moderately developed root systems and are anchored directly in the soil, most are epiphytes attached to trees or inanimate supports such as rocks, fences, cliff faces, and even electrical wires. The only bromeliad that occurs over most of the southern United States is Spanish Moss, *Tillandsia usneoides*, which grows

Bromeliads are epiphytes, deriving their nourishment and water from particles in the air, using other plants as attachment sites; they are not truly parasitic. The great variety of types, sizes, and colors available makes them suitable for almost any terrarium.

Though it may not look like a plant, Spanish Moss, *Tillandsia usneoides*, represents one of the most northern of the bromeliads. Dried strands often are used in terrarium decoration.

on trees (especially live oaks) from Virginia into Texas and southward into Mexico. This is perhaps the most unusual bromeliad, being reduced to slender, tough strings covered with thick gray scales that help absorb water and nutrients from the air. This genus contains over 400 species and is found over the entire range of the family in the Americas. Several bromeliads are common in the terrarium trade but bear little resemblance to Spanish Moss. The Pineapple, *Ananas comosus*, is the most well-known bromeliad, its unusual fruit being a gigantic berry (all the flower parts grown together) that is available canned and fresh in supermarkets at all seasons of the year.

Bromeliads are relatively primitive plants related to the arums (philodendrons, et al.). In most genera the leaves form a rosette, strap-like leaves forming whorls or spirals around a central point, the funnel. Few species seen commonly are less than 6 inches in diameter, and many are a foot or two across, with many species kept by specialists being 4 or 5 feet wide. They produce tubular flowers that may be deep within the funnel or at the end of a long stalk that may be fan-like or pyramid-like. Often the true flowers are small and almost colorless, the bright violets, reds, greens, and yellows being produced by bracts, flowerparts below the flowers. The seeds are minute and produced by the millions, often appearing like tiny cotton tufts.

The several types of readily available bromeliads are mainstays of planted terraria. Their broad, usually stiff, greenish leaves often are marked with gray and red and serve as excellent perches and hiding spots for many different types of herps, especially frogs. Some have water-holding funnels at the center of a rosette of leaves that are used by poison frogs and many other amphibians as egg-laying spots and places to raise tadpoles.

GENERAL CARE

Though bromeliads as a family may require many specialized types of care, including greenhouses and misting systems, the ones for the terrarium fall into two categories: those growable in pots and those that should be attached to branches. As a general rule, bromeliads with very stiff leaves and no water-holding funnel at the center can withstand a period of dryness but need large amounts of light, while those with lax (flexible, soft) leaves and a water-holding funnel need high humidity and less light.

Because they only need support, many *Tillandsia* and other bromeliads are tied or glued to pieces of bark and then hung down the back of the terrarium, doing quite nicely as long as they are misted frequently and kept brightly lighted. Some could even be glued directly to the glass if you wished.

Remember that all bromeliads need fresh, not stale, air to thrive.

Give bromeliads the highest light intensities that you can provide in the terrarium. Most should be elevated above the floor of the terrarium to place them closer to the center of the light. Those that do best in soil can be placed in shallow cups or depressions constructed in cork bark and hung against the back wall. A block of Styrofoam (covered with moss and lichens and painted to resemble a natural structure) or a large piece of cork bark can be placed near the center of the terrarium and the bromeliad placed on it just below the center of the lights. The true air plants, such as many *Tillandsia*, can be attached to a piece of bark or a decorative piece of driftwood by thin florist wire or even waterproof glue and suspended literally just below the lights by wires or suspended from the edges of the walls.

Bromeliads like it moist, and they should be misted every day or so if humidity in the terrarium drops significantly. Those with funnels in the center should have the water replaced at intervals of at most a week to keep the water fresh, not stagnant. If fertilizer is used, it should be weak and should be added to the water in the funnel or placed around the roots.

The soil mixture used for potting bromeliads should be loose and allow easy drainage of water. They do well in nearly sterile mixes of perlite and a little peat moss or bark chips. Those that will grow attached to branches usually do well with just a bit of long-fiber sphagnum moss wrapped around their base before the plant is attached to the branch. Potting mixes for bromeliads usually are distinctly acidic.

A word of warning about flowering bromeliads is in order. Virtually all bromeliads will produce a flower stalk or smaller flowers when they mature at about two to ten years of age. In those species that produce long, brightly colored flower stalks (many of the rosette types), the flowers mark the end of the plant's period of active growth and the beginning of its death. With few exceptions, the plant will slowly begin to fall apart, dying over a period of one or two years. This explains the large bromeliads with truly spectacular flower displays that often are available very cheaply. The flowers (actually usually the colorful bracts) may put on a show for several months.

If you realize that the flowering plant is dying, it still might be a good buy. The period following flowering and before death is when a mature bromeliad produces offshoots or pups. These first appear as small leaf balls

Aechmea fasciata is one of the most familiar urn plants, having been cultivated for going on two centuries.

near the base of the plant or between the leaves near the funnel. When they become large enough to take on the form of the adult plant, they can be removed and placed in a small pot of appropriate mix to begin their free life. One dying bromeliad may produce several viable pups.

AECHMEA—URN PLANTS OR LIVING VASES

Urn plants are large (often 2 or 3 feet in diameter and about equally high) bromeliads with a rosette of usually wide green leaves that may be banded with silver and usually have spiny edges. They have short stalks and grow well in a soilless potting mix in a pot that is watered from underneath (place the pot on a layer of pebbles or a sponge and keep this constantly moist). Additionally, they must be misted thoroughly several times a week and also taken out of the terrarium at least once a month to be fertilized with a weak liquid fertilizer in a water solution poured over the leaves and into the center funnel. In many species the center of the mature plant gradually turns reddish. The flowers are small but they are enclosed in a large oval berry with long bracts at the base.

The loosely wrapped leaves of *A. fasciata* produce an urn or phytothelm that can hold water for long periods, long enough for insects, frogs, and other animals to make a comfortable living there.

The most familiar species is *Aechmea fasciata*, which has been cultivated since 1826. It is an elegantly proportioned plant that often exceeds 2 feet in width and height and does very well in a large terrarium if kept warm and moist. The leaves are dull green with variable silvery banding and conspicuous spines at their edges. In some cultivated forms the entire leaf is silvery, the green barely being visible. Small blue flowers are produced in a large bright pink pyramid on a long pink stalk and surrounded by pink bracts. The flowers soon fall away, but the pink pyramid lasts for months. The dying adult plant may produce many pups that can be cut away when fully formed and set to grow in the same pot as the parent.

BILLBERGIA

Though they are showy bromeliads, billbergias are not common in the terrarium. They require more intense light than most setups can provide and are best adapted for growing outdoors in warm climates or in greenhouses. Unlike many other bromeliads, the flower stalks hang downward, making this an excellent plant for a basket suspended from the top of a structure. The flower head is a loose green structure with wide pink bracts. Adult plants may be over 3 feet wide. Though many species have wide deep green leaves, others have narrow grass-like leaves. Don't remove the pups until they are least 4 inches long and have well-developed roots.

The only species commonly

seen is *Billbergia nutans*, a species with grass-like leaves that is hard to kill if given sufficient light. Unfortunately the slender leaves seldom fit the terrarium decor.

CRYPTANTHUS—EARTH STARS

Several types of bromeliads produce a low rosette of leaves that literally hug the ground. One such is the familiar species of *Cryptanthus*, especially *C. zonatus*. This small plant (some cultivars and hybrids are as small as 8 inches in diameter, others may be 18 inches) produces a loose rosette of green leaves that have fine spines at the edges and are distinctly undulated (the edges go up and down like a roller coaster). The common forms are bright to dull green with much silvery banding, but cultivars may have bright pinkish to red tinges over the center of the plant and many leaf edges. The flowers are small and white and produced on a short stalk from the center; they disappear in a few days or weeks and are not showy. The pups can be allowed to detach themselves from the dying parent and then be potted in an acid mixture in a shallow pot. Earth stars require high humidities and relatively bright light to show their best colors.

DYCKIA

This is an exceptional bromeliad in that it is a succulent—its leaves are thickened and store water. It is a rather small plant only a foot or so high that does well in bright light and dry air. It has to be watered only when the soil in which it is rooted becomes almost dry. The flower stalk is erect and

Cryptanthus 'Pink Starlight' always has a reddish blush, but when exposed to bright sunlight it becomes deep red at the bases of the leaves.

Photo: B. Samples

Neoregelia species are known as blushing bromeliads because of pink to red tones at the center of the plant and the tips of the leaves. These plants almost always are sold after flowering, which means that they are dying but still are suitable for terrarium use.

in the species *D. fosterana* bears a scattering of yellow flowers near the tip. The bromeliads of this genus do not die after flowering. Unfortunately, the leaves of the *Dyckia* species bear hard, heavy spines that can puncture your fingers and might rip open a small herp. The plants are not common.

GUZMANIA

These pretty green bromeliads have long, smooth, arching leaves about a foot long. There is a central funnel from which a beautiful flower stalk 6 to 12 inches long springs during the winter months. The flowers are white and inconspicuous, but the large bracts that are below them are red and orange and last for weeks or months. Give this beautiful plant a warm, humid terrarium and put it as close to the lights as possible. It should be potted in a relatively rich, acid mixture containing peat moss and decomposing leaves. The only species commonly seen is *G. lingulata.*

NEOREGELIA—BLUSHING BROMELIADS

This colorful bromeliad is one of the most commonly seen, and it is available as several cultivars of *N. carolinae* from Brazil. These plants are large, often over 2 feet in diameter, with the bright green leaves in a tight, spreading rosette. They do well in bright light at about 75°F and are impressive terrarium plants. They are epiphytes that grow equally well in shallow pots with a mostly inorganic soil mix and tied to a sturdy branch or piece of cork and hung from a wall near the light.

Unfortunately, you won't see this plant for sale until it is dying. The flowers are small and barely

Often used in plantings in malls and other open spaces is *Guzmania lingulata*, noted for its brightly colored flower bracts. The real flowers are tiny and white, but hardly anyone notices them.

project out of the central funnel, but when they are produced (at an age of two or three years) they bring about a sudden transformation in the plant. The entire central part of the rosette becomes bright red, the color often extending well into the leaves. Several cultivars additionally have yellow or white stripes over the leaves that really accent the red central portion. Because the plants typically are sold only after the red develops, the plant will be dying before it becomes available. However, it produces a few strong pups that can be cut away from the parent plant as it falls apart and potted like the parent.

Tillandsia ionantha, **shown here fixed with hot glue to a decorative base, is a common, tiny bromeliad with widened leaf bases.**

NIDULARIUM

These small bromeliads (often only 12 to 15 inches high and wide) have an erect growth form with wide deep green leaves that arch gently from a loose rosette. They do well in typically warm, humid terrarium conditions and can live at lower light intensities than many other bromeliads. The flowers are produced in a short stalk with red to bright yellow bracts that have a very open or loose appearance. Unfortunately these attractive plants are not common.

TILLANDSIA

This gigantic genus (over 400 species) has many growth types, from the thread-like Spanish Moss to species as tall as a man and with leaves 3 feet long and an inch or more thick. The terrarium species have small root systems and do best when tied to a branch and bedded in sphagnum moss. They must be kept moist, warm, and in a system without stale air. They usually are covered with small gray scales that give all of them a distinctive appearance. The fruit is a narrow dry capsule, while the flowers may be inconspicuous and single, large and single, or produced in a large flattened, fan-like group on a long or short stalk. The species commonly seen in the terrarium hobby fall into two groups.

In the true air plants the leaves have wide bases that often overlap and are dished out and thickened, while the rest of the leaf is narrow, pointed, and often greatly twisted. These are the plants usually seen for sale at low prices already wired or glued to branches, bits of cork, or gnarly pieces of driftwood. The two most common species bear a few bright violet flowers, sometimes with

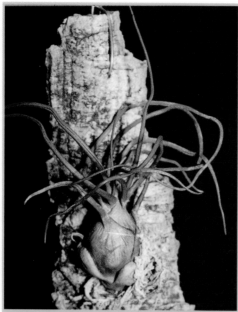

Perhaps the most bizarre common air plant is *Tillandsia caput-medusae*, noted for its onion-like base and wildly projecting leaf tips.

bright red bracts, but are grown for their leaves. The tiny *Tillandsia ionantha* has deep violet flowers that are almost as long as the rest of the plant. Mature plants are only 1.5 to 4 inches high and have moderately swollen leaf bases and narrow, twisted leaves. When flowering occurs the grayish green plant may assume a bright pink blush. The larger *T. caput-medusae* is up to a foot in height, with wide, greatly swollen leaf bases and short, erratically twisted outer ends of the leaves. It is one of the strangest bromeliads that is commonly available. The flowers are bright violet with red bracts and are large and showy. An excellent addition to any relatively warm and moist terrarium, it is easy to grow and cheap to purchase.

The other commonly seen species have narrow, grass-like leaves that are bright to dull green and may be only 10 to 14 inches long. Unlike more typical *Tillandsia*, they may lack grayish scales on the leaves, and they grow well in shallow pots as well as attached to branches. They produce a beautiful flower head of tightly overlapping bracts in two rows that are flattened, giving the entire structure a great similarity to an old-fashioned hand fan. The common *T. cyanea* has bright solid blue flowers and greenish to rosy bracts, while *T. lindenii* (the Blue Torch) has a larger flower head that may be bright blue and has blue flowers with white throats. Other species may have much more open flower heads and loose reddish bracts.

By drilling three or four holes into a cork slab, you can easily tie a *Tillandsia* onto an attractive base with monofilament line and then hang it. Wrap the base of the plant in sphagnum first to help retain moisture.

VRIESEA—SWORD BROMELIADS

The species of *Vriesea* are large (2 to 3 feet high and about as wide) plants with wide, gently curving bright green leaves that may be banded in pale brown or grayish brown. These plants are closely related to *Tillandsia* and have a flower structure somewhat similar in general shape, rather flattened with brightly colored (usually brilliant red) bracts in a few overlapping rows. They are much larger and wider-leaved than any *Tillandsia* you are likely to find in the nursery, however. *V. splendens* is known as the

The brilliant red, slender flower head (tightly closed bracts) of *Vriesea splendens* has led to the common name Flaming Sword for this familiar bromeliad.

Flaming Sword because the flower head is narrow, erect, a foot or more long, and bright red. The plants are sold when in full flower, so as you might expect the plants are beginning to die. They will hold the flower bracts for months, and it might take the parent plant two years to fall apart, leaving behind a few pups that are difficult to grow. The dying mature plants hold their form in the terrarium for a year or more and are excellent additions, serving both as hiding and resting places and a deep water funnel for egg-laying.

Vriesea splendens also is an urn plant, water accumulating in the base of the leaves, and it looks nice long after it has flowered and technically died.

CACTI AND ORCHIDS

Cacti just seem to belong in desert terraria, and every hobbyist who keeps a rainforest terrarium would love to grow an orchid or two. Actually, these two groups of plants are both so highly specialized that they are difficult to maintain in the terrarium for any period of time and are much better grown outdoors (cacti) or in a greenhouse (cacti and orchids). In fact, it is tempting to suggest that instead of purchasing a cactus you buy one or two of the truly excellent plastic models that have appeared recently in the pet shops. These will fool a casual glance, last forever, and lack spines to get into your fingers and the mouth and belly of your pet lizard.

CACTI

The family Cactaceae is a large one, with hundreds of species over the Americas. There are no native cacti in the Old World, though prickly pears (*Opuntia*) have been widely introduced into

Relatively spineless so-called "bunny ears" cacti such as *Opuntia macrodasys* are easily found and inexpensive. Few cacti survive well even in desert terraria because the air is too humid, the light too weak, and the temperature too uniform.

The common Turks Cap Cactus bears the formidable scientific name *Gymnocalycium mihanovichii*. It is a cultivated form lacking chlorophyll, so it is grafted to a different green, stronger cactus for support and nourishment.

Australia, Africa, and even the Mediterranean coast. Cacti, especially the prickly pears, range from southwestern Canada and the Long Island, New York, coast (they are common near the shore here in New Jersey) almost to the tip of South America. They range from tiny species only an inch or so high to tree-like species 40 feet high, and from spheres to tall columns and flattened "bunny ears" like most prickly pears. The leaves are reduced to tiny spines, and much of what you see actually are modified stems. There is chlorophyll in most of the tissues of the body, while the interior of the stem is supported by a meshwork of woody ribs that allow the plant to expand and contract depending on how much water has been absorbed.

These are true desert plants (with some exceptions, of course, as always) that are very specialized and thus difficult to maintain unless given very specific conditions. The root system may be a long, heavy taproot or a tremendous network covering many square yards just below the surface. They are adapted to absorb every drop of water that comes their way and hold on to it under conditions of extreme heat, dryness, and winds. The flowers tend to be large and colorful but short-lived.

Growing cacti requires a dry, loose substrate that is watered only infrequently. The humidity for the common species should be low, and if possible there should be some exposure to full sunlight each day. Obviously some of these conditions are hard to arrange in the terrarium, but it can be done. Cacti grow from the spring through the autumn, and then they need a dry rest period over the winter. If you water them in winter they probably will rot. Beware the spines, which in some forms can be a serious threat to a gangly young lizard or one more intent on food than careful footing.

If you must have cacti, try to obtain the small, almost spineless forms of *Opuntia* often sold in pet shops, variety stores, and nurseries. These probably will rot in a few months, but at least they are cheap. The gorgeous red or bright yellow Turks Cap Cactus, a cultivated mutation of

Though decorative, the many small cacti sold in plant centers usually are too spiny to be safe in the terrarium. If your lizard or snake doesn't get stuck, your hand still could become a pincushion. This is *Lobivia leucomalla* between flowers.

Gymnocalycium mihanovichii in which chlorophyll does not develop, is a virtually spineless ball that always is grafted onto a larger green cactus to support it and supply nutrition. Various species of ball-like *Ferocactus* with gigantic curved spines (often soft and not really a danger) and *Mammillaria* with hooked spines, as well as a variety of other small types, are readily available and may survive for a while.

The holiday cacti, mostly species of *Schlumbergera* (Thanksgiving), *Zygocactus* (Christmas) and *Rhipsalidopsis* (Easter), are tropical forms that are flattened and have few spines. They tolerate warm, humid terraria fairly well, though they

Hatiora salicornioides is a holiday cactus with slender, round "stems." One of my favorites, it has proved very hardy even in moist terraria and occasionally produces an abundance of bright yellow flowers.

The many-segmented "stems" of holiday cacti, here the Thanksgiving *Schlumbergera*, lack hard spines and will put out rootlets at the constrictions. These usually are difficult plants to reflower, but they survive well.

must be removed from the terrarium in order to provide a dry, dark resting period before they will flower. You might want to try purchasing a flowering specimen (cheaply) and maintaining it in the terrarium just for its form and temporary bright red to violet or white flowers. To get a specimen to flower a second time requires that you follow a carefully timed routine of several weeks or months in a cool (60°F), dark, dry area as the plant is allowed to almost dry out after the flowers fall. It then is slowly brought back to normal temperature and moisture levels and repotted, and then is put out in sunlight. Frankly, few people have much luck reflowering holiday cacti even under the best of conditions. Just enjoy one in the terrarium for a few weeks and then hope the body of the plant survives.

Closely related to the holiday cacti is *Hatiora salicornioides*, often called the Drunkard's Dream Cactus. One of my favorites, it has pencil-thin stems that are jointed every inch or two and spread in unpredictable ways from the central plant. Though it seldom flowers in the terrarium, it survives well under low to high light intensity and moderate to high humidity and provides a great plant to draw the attention of the observer.

ORCHIDS

Only a truly devoted terrarium nut would try to grow orchids in the planted terrarium. The family contains well over 25,000 species, making it perhaps the largest group of closely related living things on Earth. Though they take many different forms, typical orchids have three petals alternating with three sepals to produce the usually brightly colored flower. Typically the lower or central petal is widened and different in shape and color from the others, producing the structure called the lip or labellum. Orchids fall into two

A monopodial orchid produces flower stalks from the bases of the leaves and the stem grows continually from year to year. *Phalaenopsis* is the most common monopodial.

Look into the throat of a pretty *Phalaenopsis* hybrid to see the complicated floral structures that distinguish orchids from other flowers and aid their pollination. Moth orchids, so named from the broad-"winged" shape of the flower, are easily purchased most of the year.

broad groups, the synpodials and monopodials. In the monopodials (such as the vandas and phalaenopsis or moth orchids) there is a single stem that grows regularly from year to year and produces flower stalks from the bases of the leaves. In the synpodials (cattleyas and dendrobiums, among others) the horizontal stem stops growing during a resting period each year and the next growing season extends itself as a new segment.

Each segment produces a thick stem, a pseudobulb, that produces a leaf or leaves and the flower cluster. Many northern orchids (the family ranges from near the Arctic Circle to islands above the Antarctic Circle) form colonies of simple plants that may consist of one or two leaves and a single stem bearing one or two flowers. These simple terrestrial plants may be closely associated with fungi and will not grow unless specific fungi are present to help the seed germinate and establish its root system.

Many tropical orchids are epiphytes, the tiny seeds germinating in small deposits of soil and detritus on tree trunks and even non-living substrates. These often need high humidity and warm temperatures, but many orchids have to be kept cool (under 60°F) if they are to thrive and eventually flower. Many must be put through exacting schedules of active and inactive periods, with an alternation of wet—dry and cool—warm periods before they will flower. Many of the orchids available are produced through meristem (the growing point on a stem) culture on agar plates in sterile conditions, not by seeds.

Few orchids will live, let alone thrive, in the terrarium. One problem is that water cannot be allowed to settle on their leaves or they will die. If you must try an orchid, try a moth orchid, *Phalaenopsis*, first. These are monopodials that produce a long flower stem with many broad, flat flowers that tend toward pale pastel colors. The flowers vaguely look like the fluttery wings of moths, thus the generic and common names. Maintaining even these orchids may be difficult. They will stand the humidity and average temperatures of a woodland terrarium, but they need large drops in temperature at night. 75°F during the day and 55 to 60°F at night may be best. Water cannot be allowed to accumulate on their leaves, yet the shallow pot in which they are kept should always be moist. The potting mix has to be one of several specially made for orchids, such as osmunda (a type of fern) fiber with charcoal and unmilled peat moss added. They also need regular fertilization.

Another way to get orchids in your terrarium is much more simple: buy a specimen of a vanda, oncidium, or other colorful orchid that already is in bud. These are inexpensive and often can be maintained in a woodland terrarium at room temperatures without any special attention. In a few days to weeks they will produce one to many flowers that should last several weeks. Of course the plant probably will die after flowering because you would need a greenhouse to maintain it, but at least the beauty is there for a while.

There are many books available on both cactus and orchid culture, and some of them really should be consulted if you desperately want to grow plants from these groups. These specialized groups make great hobbies, especially if you live in a southern climate or have a greenhouse. Several societies publish journals dealing with the joys and problems of cactus and orchid growing, and there are many specialized dealers around the world that can supply almost any type of cactus or orchid that you might desire—for a price. Honestly, these two groups of plants are best thought of as separate hobbies quite remote to herpetoculture or even horticulture in general.

FOLIAGE PLANTS

A large nursery will have 100 or more types of foliage plants available almost any time of the year. Many of these are suitable for the woodland to rainforest terrarium, while some do well in drier terraria. Obviously the choice of species is broad and will vary from area to area and at different times of the year. We are talking here mostly of plants that are grown in greenhouses for the beauty of their foliage or their attractive form, as well as plants that are grown for their novelty either of appearance or some part of their life cycle.

The following short discussions try to mention most of the common (and a few uncommon) plants that adapt to the terrarium. Some are hardy and will thrive on neglect (my type of plant!), but others have cycles of active growth and dormancy that must be paid attention to if they are to survive. With one or two exceptions (African violets and begonias), none are grown for their attractive flowers, and they should not be expected to even flower in the terrarium because the light quality will be wrong or the cycling of the light is wrong in the terrarium.

Don't be afraid to talk to your pet shop manager or nursery helper about your plant needs.

Several sizes and shapes of *Acalypha* are available, some produced as hanging baskets. Though often too large and spreading for the terrarium, chenille plants or copperleafs adapt well to brightly lighted surroundings that remain warm.

The "fuzzy caterpillar" flower of *Acalypha* is one of its major distinctions, never failing to draw attention.

ACALYPHA—COPPERLEAFS, CHENILLE PLANTS

Though copperleafs may grow to 6 feet in height, they can be kept much smaller by constant pruning. These plants have oval to pointed leaves about 3 inches long that are variegated with pink to bright coppery red. They tolerate temperatures of about 80°F well and do not like drops below 60°F; they also like humid surroundings. These factors plus their bright colors make them possible terrarium plants. However, they need lots of light and seldom thrive with much less than 800 foot-candles.

A large (almost 3 feet high) variegated Chinese evergreen, *Aglaonema*. These plants survive well in warm, humid surroundings with rich soil. They even are sold as aquarium plants, though they do not live long under water.

They may be able to point you to a plant that is available cheaply in season and will do well for your specific terrarium conditions of temperature, moisture, and lighting. This chapter certainly is not an extensive listing of terrarium plants, but it should serve to give you an idea of what is out there.

The following listing is alphabetical by genus. I've tried to give common names when one or more seems to be used on a regular basis, but fortunately many plants are well known by their generic names in nursery circles. Remember that for each genus there probably is a variety of hybrids and cultivars available, and these may change (both in availability and names) from year to year.

ADIANTUM—MAIDENHAIR FERNS

These beautiful spreading, bright green to yellow-green ferns often have distinctively rounded leaflets. Several species are available. Like many other ferns, they do well at average room temperatures and moderate light, plus they have a need for high humidity. These factors make them well-suited to the moist woodland terrarium. They have to dry out a bit during the winter, however, and are best removed from the terrarium then and stored in a cool, dry area and given minimal watering. In the spring divide the rhizome (assuming the plant grew well the previous year) and repot your plants in a good potting soil with peat moss added.

Aglaonemas come in many sizes and colors. This particular plant was only a foot high, with solid green leaves. These plants do very well in many amphibian terraria.

AGLAONEMA—CHINESE EVERGREENS

These hardy members of the arum family are familiar broad-leaved plants that do well in very low light situations. Like other arums, they like moist, warm situations, though the soil in which they are potted should be a bit on the dry side. They should be shaded by other plants and not exposed to the brightest center of the lights. In the common *A. costatum* the plant seldom grows higher than a foot and 18 inches across, but each leaf may be 6 inches long and 3 inches wide. The midrib is white, the rest of the leaf green but speckled and mottled with much white. In some of the cultivars the leaves are mostly white. Other species may grow to 40 inches in height and have less white mottling on the leaves. Most have inconspicuous flower stalks, but some have bright red berries (though they seldom will flower in the terrarium). Highly recommended.

ALOCASIA—ELEPHANT EARS

Many of the arums from the tropics have large leaves that look great in a very large rainforest terrarium. *Alocasia* is one of the several forms known as elephant ears because the leaves are broad at the base and taper to a long point. In this genus the whitish midrib produces a distinct Y, the leaf is bright shiny green, and there are many heavy ribs off the main rib. They must be kept moist (though the soil should be dried a bit during the winter), humid, and warm (not below

Kris Plants or Elephant Ears, *Alocasia amazonica*, grow too large for most terraria, but the distinctive leaf shape and coloration are draws for the more daring keeper.

The spathe (true flowers plus bract) of *Caladium hortulanum*, the Angelwings, is similar to that of most other aroid plants. Few of these plants flower readily in the terrarium or even the greenhouse.

Though growing large, the Angelwings is an attractive temporary addition to the humid terrarium. Many colors are available, from white to flaming red, and some stay relatively small for quite a while. Unfortunately, the plants die back to the tuber in the fall.

65°F). A plant probably will not live well in a terrarium for very long, and if it does thrive it will outgrow almost any enclosure. It's worth a try, however, if you want a very dramatic plant. Angelwings, *Caladium*, are very similar and perhaps easier to find, but they die back completely to the tuber during the autumn.

ALOE—ALOES

Everyone knows the common kitchen aloe, *Aloe vera* or perhaps *A. barbadensis*, that is kept around to rub on burns and blisters. They are succulents, with thickened leaves that end in sometimes sharp points and usually have spines along the edges. Their bright green leaves

There are many *Aloe* forms available that lack spines on the leaves or have just small teeth. Look for these if you want to add the genus to the backdrop in your terrarium.

A common *Aloe* displaying vicious spines along the leaf edges. Such spines really are able to disembowel a small lizard carelessly jumping after food, so this is not a safe addition to the terrarium.

often are variegated with white or silver, and some have red spines. Most do well in a dry terrarium with good lighting and moderate to low humidity, plus average room temperatures. They are tolerant of extreme conditions for a while and may grow to 1 to 2 feet in height indoors. Species with weak or fleshy spines are best for the terrarium because they are easier to handle and less likely to cause accidents.

ANTHURIUM—FLAMINGO PLANTS

This staple of the florist trade is grown for its large bright green leaves and brilliant red spathes below the curly flower stalk that looks a bit like a red or white rat's tail. The plants most commonly seen are various hybrids and cultivars of *A. scherzerianum*, but other species occasionally are seen. A more beautiful addition to the terrarium can hardly be

Anthurium scherzerianum 'Taffy' is one of the smaller flamingo plants, but it still has a nice red bract around the cob-like flower, producing a distinctive spathe. The spathe is tough and will last for weeks even if the plant is in poor shape.

imagined, but they are difficult to maintain in the confines of the terrarium. They need constant heat (80's F), high humidity, moist soil, and bright but somewhat shaded surroundings. The red flowers last for weeks or months, and even a dying plant will be useful for quite a while.

ASPIDISTRA—CAST-IRON PLANT

Though it may grow to 3 feet in height, this member of the lily family may make a great addition to the woodland terrarium. The thin, tough leaves come up individually (there is no main stem) from the pot and are bright green, wide, and pointed. They do well under moderately low light and shaded conditions and can tolerate a lot of dirty air and dust. The main terrarium problem is

The tough, bright green leaves of a flamingo plant look good in any larger terrarium, but this admittedly is a difficult plant to keep for very long. Give your *Anthurium* frequent rests in a shaded, humid, warm environment.

that they don't like humid situations and high temperatures. They are most comfortable at average room temperatures, so you cannot use them in a strongly heated terrarium. The soil of their pot should be fairly dry, never moist. If your terrarium meets these requirements, give the plant a try.

ASPLENIUM—SPLEENWORTS

These broad-leaved ferns are great for the woodland terrarium, liking its moderate temperatures, high humidity, and low light (but preferably 200 foot-candles or more). Their leaves are rather delicate, however, and can be torn by the animals. Bird's-nest Fern, *A. nidus*, often is available and may grow to 2 to 3 feet in height under the best conditions and likes moist soil.

BEGONIA—BEGONIAS

With over 1,000 species and another 10,000 hybrids and cultivars, this is one of the largest genera of plants, and there is no such thing as a "typical" begonia. Common pot begonias grown for their flowers also have rounded bright green leaves and bear white to reddish flowers on long erect stalks. Some grow well from hanging baskets, and all tolerate a high degree of humidity in the air, but they don't like wet soil. They all like bright light, so it may be to your advantage to elevate their pots toward the center of the lights. If you purchase flowering specimens in the spring, they may continue to flower for several weeks or months, but the light levels in the terrarium probably will be too low to permit further flowering. Great looking plants

Few ferns are sturdy enough to survive in the reptile terrarium, being torn apart by the movements and occasional nibbles of the animals. Bird's-nest Fern, *Asplenium nidus*, is so attractive that it often is given a try, however, and it will do well with small frogs.

Though common begonias, usually *Begonia tuberhybrida*, make poor terrarium plants, their bright flowers hold for several weeks and the plants are easily and inexpensively replaced.

More unusual and expensive begonias, such as *Begonia argenteo-guttata*, one of the cane-stemmed begonias, can be tried in the terrarium, but be prepared for losses.

that are cheap and easy to care for, they also are very easy to find almost anywhere.

CALATHEA—ZEBRA PLANTS

The 15-inch bright green *Calathea zebrina* is a hardy, attractive broad-leaved plant that is easy to grow in moist surroundings at room temperature and moderate light (400 foot-candles). The rounded leaves appear finely veined and are pale green with dark green stripes above, purplish below. Not always easy to find, it certainly is worth a try.

CEROPEGIA—ROSARY VINES

This attractive and distinctive vine looks good draped over a wall or going up a trellis in a corner. Purplish stems that can reach 3 feet in length grow from a large tuber that can store a lot of water. The leaves are widely spaced, only a half inch or so wide, silvery green above and purplish below. The plant grows well at average room temperatures and humidity, but it needs at least 400 foot-candles of light and thus a fairly bright terrarium placement. Let the soil in its pot go almost dry before watering.

CHLOROPHYTUM—SPIDER PLANTS

This traditional house plant has long, narrow pale green leaves with a broad whitish central stripe. It does well at average temperatures, humidities, and moderate light. Because its rootstock stores water, its pot should be allowed to become almost dry before watering. When it becomes pot-bound it sends out

A Spider Plant pup. These are produced at the end of long runners and, when broken off and placed on moist soil, rapidly root and begin to grow. One good Spider Plant can produce dozens of pups over a season.

Spider Plants, *Chlorophytum comosum*, are cheap and extremely hardy plants noted for their pupping behavior. They do well under average conditions, though too much water can hurt them.

long runners that produce baby plants at their ends. Under the proper conditions it can take over a small area in just a few months. It is worth trying and easy to find.

CISSUS—KANGAROO VINES, GRAPE IVYS

These hanging basket plants are easy to grow if kept on the cool side and given moderate to bright light. They produce grape-like tendrils that they use to climb, and good specimens will reach several feet in length if not pinched back regularly. The leaves usually are bright green and commonly have irregular edges, but there is much variation in the group. *C. antarctica*, the Kangaroo Vine, is from Australia and has weakly serrated (saw-toothed) leaves, while *C. rhombifolia*, the true Grape Ivy, has deeply cut bright shiny green leaves. If you don't let their soil get too moist, they should do fine in the woodland terrarium.

CRASSULA—JADE PLANTS

The familiar Jade Plant, *Crassula portulacea*, is a standard succulent familiar to everyone. Though the thick stems are dark brown, the rounded 2-inch leaves are bright green. Unfortunately, the leaves are weakly attached to the stems and easy to knock off, perhaps the major disadvantage of the Jade Plant. Though it prefers bright light, it survives well in moderate light if taken out of the terrarium on a regular basis and put outdoors to relax. Allow the soil to become almost dry before watering. Jade Plants do moderately well in a dry terrarium, especially if put below

the center of the lights.

CYRTOMIUM—HOLLY FERNS

These bright green spreading ferns can tolerate dry air, low temperatures, and low light conditions. They may be virtually indestructible unless trampled by the animals. The soil should be kept fairly moist at all times, and the plant should be washed off occasionally. They need a rich potting mix with lots of peat moss and some bone meal added as a supplement. Though they like low light (150 foot-candles), they don't like to be shaded.

DIEFFENBACHIA—DUMB CANES

Small dieffenbachias look very nice in the terrarium and survive fairly well at low humidity and room temperature. They need about 400 foot-candles of light to be comfortable, and they should be watered when their soil

Jade Plants, *Crassula portulacea* (sometimes called *C. argentea*), are among the most familiar succulents, plants with thickened leaves to store water. Unfortunately, their leaves are easily knocked off the stem, so they cannot be used in areas with much activity.

Though attractive, the leaves of *Dieffenbachia picta* and other species of the genus contain crystals of oxalic acid that can cause mechanical damage to the lips, gums, and throat of any animal taking a bite. This genus is too dangerous to use in the terrarium.

Though not stunning, the Ribbon Plant, *Dracaena sanderiana*, forms an interesting background piece for a larger terrarium.

Gold-dust Plants, *Dracaena surculosa* (formerly *D. godseffiana*), are distinctive and hardy if given sufficient light and not exposed to excessive humidity. The tough leaves are excellent perches for small herps.

becomes almost dry. However, they have two disadvantages. Their leaves, which may reach 18 inches long, may come out of a stem that reaches 5 or 6 feet in height. When purchased they may be only a foot or 18 inches high, but they soon will outgrow most terraria. Additionally, their sap contains oxalic acid crystals that, if eaten by an iguana or other animal, may cause swelling of the mouth and throat and possible suffocation. Use them at your own risk.

DRACAENA—DRAGON PLANTS

Though they are related to the aloes, dragon plants do not look like succulents. Their leaves and general form vary greatly from one species to the next, but the most common types look a lot like corn plants (and one species, *D. fragrans* 'Massangeana,' commonly is sold as the Corn Plant), with broad, bright green leaves coming from a tall central stem. Unfortunately, most dragon plants grow to 5 or 6 feet in height and are much too large for typical terraria. One species, *D. surculosa* (formerly *D. godseffiana*), the Gold-dust Plant, is only 18 inches high and has large leaves coming from a branching main stem; the leaves are bright green with, as you expect, gold dustings. Keep all these plants in moderately bright light (at least 400 foot-

Houseleeks (hens and chicks), *Sempervivum*, are cheap and hardy and often quite colorful. They do well in rocky, brightly lighted terraria but can withstand higher humidity for at least a while. Beware the sharp spines at the tips of the leaves, however.

candles) and at normal room temperatures and humidities.

ECHEVERIA—ECHEVERIAS

These are familiar succulents that usually form dense rosettes of thick green to gray-green leaves low on the ground. Some species have red in the leaves, and any may produce bright white to red flowers on an erect stalk. They do fairly well in the desert terrarium, especially if they can have cool nighttime temperatures and bright light (preferably at least a few hours of 800 foot-candles each day). Even plants that do not adapt well will live for quite a while in a dry terrarium. They need a dry period during the winter, but should be watered before the leaves shrivel too badly.

Common, cheap, and very attractive plants, they are worth a try in any desert terrarium. Houseleeks or hens and chicks, *Sempervivum*, are even more common and just as hardy in rocky terraria, though types with a sharp spine at the tip of each leaf could cause problems.

EPISCIA—CARPET PLANTS

These hothouse plants are noted for their oval, fuzzy leaves and bright red flowers. They do well in shaded conditions and high temperatures, but they must always be kept in humid air. This would make them good possibilities for the rainforest terrarium, but they cannot stand to have water on their leaves, which means that they cannot

One of the most stunning plants to try in the humid terrarium is a Carpet Plant, *Episcia cupreata*. Though the red flowers soon drop off, the textured leaves survive well if water is not allowed to accumulate on their surface. Water these plants from the bottom.

take the regular spraying typical of rainforest terraria. Relatives of the African violets, they are not easy to find.

EUPHORBIA—SPURGES

If you've seen a poinsettia, you've seen a spurge. The genus is a gigantic one that takes many forms, but the ones suitable for the terrarium generally look like various types of cacti and may have large spines. Some are small globes, while others are tall stalks with wide ridges or flanges. Their sap is milky and often causes local toxic reactions in some people and animals. They may survive for a while in desert terraria, but like most succulents they need bright light that may be

Small *Euphorbia* with few or no spines are easily available and can be tried in the desert or savanna terrarium. Give them a spotlight for the best chances of survival.

hard to duplicate in the home. Some forms are so bizarre in appearance, however, that they are hard to pass by if cheap enough.

FICUS—RUBBER TREES, ORNAMENTAL FIGS

Though the various types of rubber trees are too large for the typical terrarium, the broad, bright green leaves, often with purple undersides, always draw attention and figs often are placed in the terrarium anyway. They like relatively bright light and soil that is not too moist, but are quite tolerant of most conditions. Many plants will allow drastic pruning each spring, often returning after the stem is cut down to only a few inches above the soil. The leaves get dirty very easily because everything likes to perch on them, and they should be washed often.

Though they may look like cacti, spurges (here the large *Euphorbia heterochroma*) really are related to the milkweeds. Beware the sticky white sap—many people (and perhaps herps) are allergic to it. The plants need bright light and relatively dry conditions.

Yes, this really is a fig, the Creeping Fig, *Ficus pumila*. *Ficus* is one of the large genera of plants with a tremendous variety of appearances, from herbs and vines to trees. Creeping Figs are very tolerant plants but will be eaten by some herbivores.

The Rubber Plant, *Ficus elastica*, probably is the most familiar household fig, but its large size makes it tough to adapt to a terrarium. If you keep cutting off the top, however, you can produce a short stem with just a few wide leaves.

Weeping Figs, *Ficus benjamina*, are recognizable by their narrow, long-tipped leaves and drooping posture. The leaves of these small trees are edible, which is a problem if you are keeping an iguanid—or maybe an answer to the "what do I feed it" question.

Ornamental figs with smaller, more normal leaves, such as Weeping Fig, *Ficus benjamina*, today often are used in the large enclosures that house chameleons and similar sedentary lizards. These are the small trees you often notice in pots in the corners of restaurants and offices, so they obviously are very hardy. To get sufficient light, however, you may have to place a spotlight to illuminate each plant—but the chameleons might enjoy that too.

FITTONIA

Perhaps some of the best background plants for the rainforest terrarium, fittonias actually come from the rain forests of Peru. They need heat, constant high humidity, and low light (150 foot-candles) in a shaded area. Most grow to only 8 inches in height and have leaves 2 to 4 inches long, oval, various shades of green, and very deeply and prominently veined with red or silver. As long as their soil is not absolute mud, they should do well.

GASTERIA

The gasterias are succulents from southern Africa that have a distinctive growth form, the dark green, fleshy leaves growing in alternation from a central axis. The leaves may be pointed or blunt, tapered to the tip or with parallel sides, and solid green or heavily spotted with pale green and silvery green. Most are only 4 to 6 inches high. They like moderate to bright light, dry and warm surrounding, and are hard

One of the neatest plants for the rainforest terrarium is *Fittonia*, here the variety 'Stripes Forever.' The strongly patterned leaves make an excellent background, and the plant's relatively small size and adaptability to high humidity and stagnant air are strong points in its favor.

The Star Window Plant, *Haworthia tessellata*, gets it name from the overall shape plus the presence of translucent "panes" in the leaves to facilitate photosynthesis. This species usually lacks the strong leaf-tip spine of other wart plants.

Haworthia margaritifera, the Pearl Plant, has the "warts" strongly developed and a contrasting white color. This is one of the more common succulents sold in any large plant center, and it does fairly well in dry terraria.

to kill. Excellent filler plants in the desert terrarium, they are easy to find and inexpensive.

HAWORTHIA—WART PLANTS

Haworthias look like small aloes studded with rows of large white warts. Some types have spines on the sides of the green to brownish leaves, and most have a large spine at the tip of each leaf (which you might prefer to cut off). They like bright, warm, dry surroundings and are easy to maintain. Water them sparingly after they have become completely dry and show signs of shriveling. They are excellent background plants in the desert terrarium, but some people are afraid of their spines. The common Zebra

Most *Hoya* are noted for their brilliant flowers, but the little *Hoya bella* 'rubra' is small enough to be tried in the woodland terrarium. You probably will have to remove it to cool surroundings in the winter, however.

Though they are not especially easy to maintain, *Lithops* will survive for quite some time in a dry terrarium when given its own spotlight.

Haworthia, *H. fasciata*, is bright green with whitish bands and grows only 4 to 6 inches high. Add bone meal to their potting mix.

HOYA—WAX FLOWERS

These familiar climbing plants are grown for their waxy green leaves and large clusters of brightly colored small flowers. They have to be kept cool during the winter, but could be added to the terrarium for a while just to add color. They really are not great terrarium plants.

LITHOPS—LIVING STONES

There are few plants that are more bizarre than living stones. They are tiny plants that consist of two thick leaves that fuse

Living stones, *Lithops* sp., are unique plants adapted to deserts of southern Africa. The pattern on the surface controls the entry of light into the plant, which likes it very bright but relatively cool. The entire body of the plant consists of two fused leaves.

together over most of their length, leaving only a variable slit at the top of the plant. In *Lithops* there is a deep cleft between the two leaves that is easily visible along the sides; in the related *Conophytum* there is only a small slit across the top of the plant to mark where the leaves fused. These are low-growing plants only an inch or so high and various shades of green to silvery green. They like bright light and very dry conditions but do quite well in a desert terrarium, especially if a spotlight is used to increase the light. Oddly, they do not like very hot temperatures. Amazingly, these strange plants often are inexpensive and as such are worth trying.

MARANTA—PRAYER PLANTS

These beautiful and odd little (sometimes only 6 to 8 inches high, with oval leaves 3 or 4 inches long) plants need warm temperatures and high humidities, so they often do well in rainforest terraria. Keep their soil moist except during the winter, when they should be allowed to dry out a bit. The leaves are deeply veined and bright green with red spots and netting, and some cultivars may have yellow and silvery highlights. The common name refers to the leaves slowly becoming erect, like praying hands, when the lights are turned off. Give them at least 150 foot-candles of light and keep them shaded.

Prayer Plants, *Marantha tricolor*, usually are sold as hanging baskets, and their broad leaves are admittedly weak. However, the bright colors offset minor inconveniences, and they are worth a try in the woodland terrarium.

The underside of a leaf of *Marantha tricolor* displays an elaborate pattern of red and green (and sometimes yellow) as well as very strong veins. If not kept humid, the leaves often dry at the tips.

MONSTERA—SWISS CHEESE PLANT

This giant philodendron has circular to elongated leaves often a foot long and bearing slits and holes in the adult form (thus the common name). Young plants look like normal philodendrons, the holes developing with age. They are harder to maintain than regular philos but may be worth the effort in a large terrarium. They are climbing vines with long roots that tend to look for water. Provide moderately bright light and warm, humid surroundings. The soil mix should have bone meal or limestone added. Too big for most terraria, it will grow to 6 feet or more if allowed to get out of control. Though the root contains a toxin, it is considered good eating in the tropics if properly prepared, thus the

One of the more attractive peperomias is *Peperomia caperata* 'Redleaf Ripple,' noted for its deeply veined leaves and red stems. These are hardy plants in woodland terraria.

Peperomia obtusifolia bears little resemblance to *P. caperata* and often is called the Baby Rubber Plant. The deep green leaves like fairly bright light.

scientific name *Monstera deliciosa.*

PEPEROMIA

This is another large and varied genus of low-growing foliage plants that do well under woodland terrarium conditions. If the soil is not kept too moist, they do well at room temperatures and moderate light. The leaves are bright green, usually variegated with yellow, red, or dark green, and they tend to be thick and shiny. Some forms have deeply veined leaves. In the common types the stems are red, and they produce an erect white flower stalk that looks a bit like a magician's wand. Many types are available cheaply and are worth experimenting with.

The Heart-leaved Philodendron or Sweetheart Plant, *Philodendron scandens*, is perhaps the most useful terrarium plant, requiring very little care, spreading rapidly, and adapting to many different keeping conditions.

PHILODENDRON

Though this large genus of climbing rainforest plants has many species and types in the nursery trade, the Heart-leaved Philodendron, *Philodendron scandens*, is the most familiar and easiest species to grow. It needs moderate light, room temperatures, and can take humid or dry air. Because it is a climber with large aerial roots, it usually is trained to grow up a slab of bark or a peat-moss-filled wire climbing log. This is a species that will grow in water if the aerial roots are allowed to spread outward and look for drier substrates. This species has bright, shiny green leaves with long pointed tips and a distinctly heart-shaped leaf, especially in young plants. Philodendrons of various types often form the basis of the plantings for many different types of woodland to relatively dry rainforest terraria. More unusual types may have purple foliage or broad, deeply cut leaves growing from a central rootstock.

PILEA—ALUMINUM PLANTS

These peculiar little plants, especially *P. cadierei*, are about 6 to 10 inches tall and have leaves 3 inches long. The leaves have three very deeply impressed veins and look oddly quilted, plus they seem to have been brushed with aluminum paint. Other species

Though considered an "old fashioned" house plant, *Pilea cadierei*, the Aluminum Plant, still is one of the hardiest and most interesting plants for a woodland terrarium, as long as it is not overburdened by active lizards and snakes.

may have coppery or bright green leaves. They do well in warm, moderately bright surroundings but should not be kept too moist. Hard to kill and very pretty, they also are inexpensive and easy to find.

SAINTPAULIA—AFRICAN VIOLETS

Saintpaulia ionantha originally came from East Africa and today has become one of the most familiar flowering plants sold in the spring. Their care sometimes is complicated (they hate calcium, for instance, and cannot be sprayed or watered with regular water), but the plants available today are relatively hardy hybrids that can survive in dry air and moderate temperatures. They

need fairly bright light to prosper, however, which means they seldom do well in the terrarium. There are many forms that differ in leaf and flower colors, sizes, and structure, but most have rounded, rather thick dark green leaves that grow in a rosette from a central point. The flowers tend to be white, red, or purple and are produced in abundance from rather long stalks. To keep them in the terrarium, provide temperatures in the 70's F, constantly moist air, and the brightest fluorescent lights you can get (or just elevate the plants to a position under the lights). Water occasionally with warm, demineralized water, trying not to get any on the leaves. You might

Once widely known as the Friendship Plant (easy to maintain and hard to kill), *Pilea involucrata* looks little like the related Aluminum Plant. This variety, 'Moon Valley,' has strongly textured leaf surfaces.

Snake plants, here *Sansevieria trifasciata*, are hardy and available in a variety of sizes and conformations. Those with short, wide leaves ending in a sharp spine once were known as "mother-in-law's tongues," an epithet now perhaps best forgotten. They are a great plant for many terrarium situations and are easy to find.

have better luck just adding flowering plants to the terrarium each spring and replacing them yearly.

SANSEVIERIA—SNAKE PLANTS

Snake plants are among the hardiest of terrarium plants and are hard to kill (they survive even my "black thumb"). Typically they are 6 to 18 inches high and consist of a group of rather broad, thick leaves that grow around a central point to produce a funnel at the center. Each leaf ends in a long, sharp spine (leading to the politically incorrect name mother-in-law's tongue) but has smooth edges. Typically they are pale to

dark green, strongly and irregularly banded in very pale green to whitish, often with yellow edges to the leaves. If you don't drown them by over-watering, they will take almost any type of temperature and soil that you throw at them, but remember that they basically are desert plants and therefore do best if warm, dry, and brightly lighted. Their pot should have a drain hole and a good layer of pebbles and clay shards to assure proper drainage. You can't go wrong with snake plants in anything from the desert to the moderately humid woodland terrarium.

SCINDAPSUS—POTHOS, DEVIL'S IVYS

Devil's ivys and pothos are plants that are much like *Philodendron* in appearance and botanically are hard to tell apart without looking at the details of flower structure. Unfortunately, these plants seldom flower under household conditions. Like philodendrons they are climbing vines with large aerial roots and somewhat heart-shaped leaves. The leaves are deep green, yellow-green below, and are lightly to heavily sprinkled with yellowish to whitish spots. The Common Pothos is *Scindapsus aureus*, also widely known as *Epipremnum aureum* or *Rhaphidophora aurea*. It is not quite as hardy as common philodendrons and grows a bit slower, but it still can overgrow a terrarium if given the chance. The thin bracts surrounding the petioles (leaf stalks) often are sharply bent near

Golden Pothos, *Scindapsus aureus*, often is sold as just another philodendron, and admittedly the two plants are difficult to tell apart without flowers. Very hardy in the home and terrarium, it seldom flowers, of course increasing the confusion of proper identification.

the tips. Forms with bright green leaves and little pale speckling can tolerate moderate light, but cultivars with mostly pale leaves need brighter lighting. The plants do well under normal conditions of temperature, moisture, and air humidity, but they do best if potted in an acid mix and trained to climb a peat-moss-filled wire log. Pothos is said to be one of the main plants eaten by the Solomons Monkey Skink, *Corucia zebrata*, and the plant is indeed native to the Solomons.

SPATHIPHYLLUM—PEACE LILIES

In many ways spathiphyllums are excellent plants for the large, moist terrarium. They have long, broad, deep green leaves on long stalks and provide excellent resting places for amphibians.

However, the leaves are rather thin and lose a lot of water through evaporation, so they must be in constantly humid air and the soil in their pot must be kept moist. During the winter growth slows and they can be dried out a bit. Most species are about 1 to 2 feet high, but they spread aggressively and may come to occupy a large area. The crowning glory of the plant is the flower, which consists of a whitish or yellow "cob" and a large shiny white bract (the spathe) at the base. Usually the flower stalks (there may be several per plant) extend well above the leaves, making them even more conspicuous. After about a week the white bract turns greenish, and the flower may be attractive for over a month. In many ways peace lilies look like flamingo plants (*Anthurium*) with white instead of red flower bracts. These beautiful plants often are sold as aquarium plants and may be easy to find in pet shops.

TRADESCANTIA—SPIDERWORTS

Spiderworts are trailing plants from the Americas that often are grown in hanging baskets. They consist of numerous thin, segmented stems (runners) and slender, pointed, paired leaves. The plants are fairly succulent and don't have to be watered

The slender stems of spiderworts, here the common *Tradescantia virginiana*, won't tolerate much abuse, but the plants spread rapidly and produce excellent flowers under moist conditions.

Peace lilies are great plants for the larger terrarium where they can be kept in humid air. The broad green leaves and large white (later green) spathes are distinctive. This is *Spathiphyllum wallisii*, one of the smaller forms.

regularly, but they also tolerate humid surroundings. Where the runners touch soil they tend to develop roots and can be pinched off to develop new plants. Though they would prefer fairly strong light, they will tolerate lower light conditions for at least a while. During the winter they should be kept a bit drier. Rapidly growing plants may need to be fertilized every two weeks or so (remove them from the terrarium for this). The Wandering Jew, *Zebrina pendula*, is very similar but typically has even more variegated leaves.

The about 60 plants covered in this book are of course just an introduction to the subject of terrarium plants, and you should feel free to experiment with interesting plants that strike your fancy and would be no great disaster to your budget if you should happen to lose them. The diversity of potential terrarium plants is high, and many types will have a great future in American terraria.